A refresher course!

RESTART® GUITAR

Wise Publications
part of The Music Sales Group
London / New York / Paris / Sydney / Copenhagen / Berlin / Madrid / Hong Kong / Tokyo

T0085585

Published by
Wise Publications
14-15 Berners Street, London W1T 3LJ, UK.

Exclusive Distributors:
Music Sales Limited
Distribution Centre, Newmarket Road,
Bury St Edmunds, Suffolk IP33 3YB, UK.

Music Sales Corporation
180 Madison Avenue, 24th Floor, New York NY 10016, USA.

Music Sales Pty Limited
Units 3-4, 17 Willfox Street, Condell Park,
NSW 2200, Australia.

Order No. AM1008073
ISBN: 978-1-78305-824-2
This book © Copyright 2014 Wise Publications,
a division of Music Sales Limited.

Edited by Toby Knowles
Cover designed by Paul Tippett
Book designed by Chloë Alexander Design
Photography by Matthew Ward
Guitar played by Barney Muller
Audio recorded, mixed and mastered by Imogen Hall
Model: Tony Jones

Printed in the EU

Your Guarantee of Quality
As publishers, we strive to produce every book to the highest
commercial standards.

This book has been carefully designed to minimise awkward page
turns and to make playing from it a real pleasure.

Particular care has been given to specifying acid-free, neutral-
sized paper made from pulps which have not been elemental
chlorine bleached. This pulp is from farmed sustainable forests
and was produced with special regard for the environment.
Throughout, the printing and binding have been planned to
ensure a sturdy, attractive publication which should give years of
enjoyment.

If your copy fails to meet our high standards, please inform us
and we will gladly replace it.

www.musicsales.com

Contents

Refresh Your Guitar Skills!

Maybe you used to play when you were younger. Perhaps you regret giving up. Don't worry — help is at hand! This book has been devised to reintroduce you to that guitar you put in storage, or — if you no longer have it — to encourage you to get a new one and rediscover the pleasures of playing.

A new start

Depending on your skill level, starting again can bring several benefits. This book concentrates on steel string guitars, both acoustic and electric. (Some advice applies to nylon string guitars as well, but this is not a classical guitar book and you may need to look for a more specialised book if that is where your ambitions lie). So first decide whether you want to refresh acoustic or electric guitar skills, or both. Next, take a good look at the instrument you're planning to use.

An Existing Guitar

Check that any guitar that has been stored for a long time has not warped. The neck in particular should not be bowed. Some guitars have a truss rod built into the neck that allows you to correct minor distortions with an adjuster usually hidden behind a plate just above the nut. If all appears well, it may anyway a good idea to put on a new set of strings before you start. This will often brighten the sound as old strings can sound dead and may even have touches of rust (see page 60).

A New Guitar

It may be a good idea to buy a new guitar. It does not have to be expensive but the reason many young guitarists give up is because their first guitar had poor action making the strings unnecessarily hard to hold down cleanly. You do not want any extra obstacles so give yourself the best chance of success by choosing both the style quality of guitar that will give you the results you want. A music shop should be able to advise you on the best instrument for you.

Ready To Go!

Depending on your skill level you can start at the beginning of this book or skip to a section where you feel more comfortable. Practice is important. Never try to advance beyond a level that you have not yet mastered. Most of all, have fun and learn to play the way you always wanted to!

Your guitar

Acoustic

- headstock
- tuning pegs
- nut
- frets
- fingerboard
- strings
- body
- soundhole
- bridge

Electric

- tuning pegs
- headstock
- nut
- frets
- fingerboard
- strap pin
- body
- strings
- bridge
- volume/tone controls
- pickup selector

Know your guitar

Tip

Looking after your guitar
When not being played, try to keep your guitar in its case, away from heat and direct sunlight, where it can't be knocked over. Keep it in a room where the temperature is relatively constant.

The headstock (at the end of the fretboard) has six tuning pegs, either three each side or all six in a row.

The tuning pegs – or machine heads – consist of a metal capstan and a cog, and are used to adjust the tension of the strings.

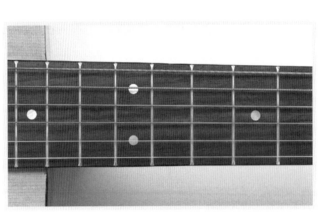

The strings traverse the fretboard which may have plastic or tortoiseshell inlays to help you see where you are on the neck. There are dots on the side of the neck at given fret positions as well.

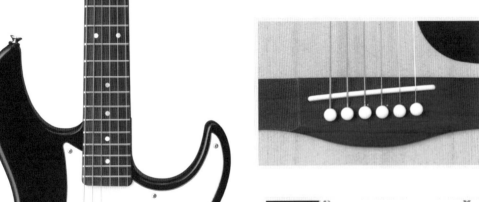

The strings are attached to the body at the bridge, which comes in all shapes and sizes depending on the guitar. It acts to alter the 'action' of the guitar.

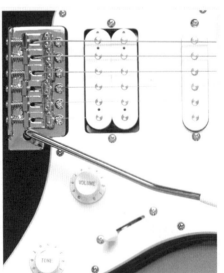

Below the strings and bridge, most electric guitars have controls for volume and tone as well as a pickup selector. It's a good idea to experiment with the different pickups and volume / tone knobs straight away, as different combinations will produce quite different sounds.

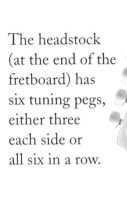

Tuning your guitar

It is essential that you tune your guitar accurately, although it may take some practice before you can do so confidently. The easiest way to tune your guitar will be by using an electronic tuner, phone app or tuning software. However, there are a few more traditional methods which are useful to know.

Tuning to the piano

If you have a piano or keyboard at home, you can tune each string individually to the relevant note on the piano. The diagram below shows the pitch of each string, as you would play it on the piano.

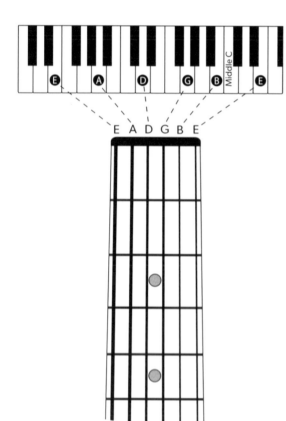

The principle is the same if you are tuning to any other instrument, or to pitch pipes: play the piano note, and twist the machine head up and down until the open guitar string matches it.

Tip

When tuning, it is always better to tune up to the correct pitch rather than down. Therefore, if you find that the pitch of the string is higher (or 'sharper') than the correct pitch, you should wind the string down below the correct pitch, and then tune up to it.

Relative Tuning

Assuming that your thick E string (string 6) isn't too out of tune, you can tune to the guitar 'to itself', by tuning each string to the one below it.

While checking the various positions on the diagram below, place a finger from your left hand on:

The 5th fret of the thick E string and tune the open A (5th string) to this note.

The 5th fret of the A string and tune the open D (4th string) to this note.

The 5th fret of the D string and tune the open G (3rd string) to this note.

The 4th fret of the G string and tune the open B (2nd string) to this note.

The 5th fret of the B string and tune the open E (1st string) to this note.

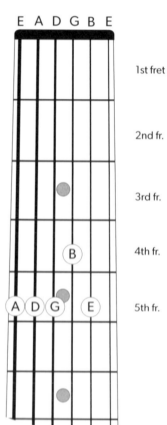

Remember that it is the open string that you are altering – not the fretted note.

This method relies on your thick E string being in tune, so it is useful to have a reference tone for the note E.

Did you know that *Led Zeppelin I* opens with an E chord? Putting the record on or even 'remembering' that sound in your head will provide a useful reference tone.

Holding the guitar

Following some simple guidelines will ensure that you always feel comfortable when playing the guitar.

1 Your arms should never take the weight of the guitar; they should be free just to play it.

2 Always keep the neck pointing slightly above the horizontal. Never let it point down towards the ground.

3 If you stand, you should not be supporting the guitar. Adjust the strap so the guitar is at a sensible height and position it so there is an equal balance of weight. When you take your hands away it should sit comfortably.

4 When practising, it's more comfortable to sit down. If you play right handed, you will want to rest the guitar on your right thigh, and again make sure that the neck is not pointing downwards.

Holding the pick

The pick is held between the thumb and index finger of your strumming hand. Try out a few sizes and thicknesses of pick to find one you're comfortable with. Hold the pick securely and don't have too much of it protruding from your fingers towards the strings.

Pick each string individually, using downstrokes.

At first the pick may seem awkward, but this feeling will fade, and it will become like an extension of your hand.

Play the open strings one at a time from the 6th to the 1st, then from the 5th to the 1st, 4th to the 1st and so on. Your pick should be hitting the upper side of each string and travelling toward the floor. This is known as a *downstroke*. If you reverse this action, strumming upwards, you will play an *upstroke*.

Now try strumming across the strings with the pick – down and up. If you remember how to play an E chord then hold it down with the left hand, otherwise just play open strings. The idea is to get used to the sensation of the pick travelling across the strings.

Tip

Different picks

In broad terms, there are three types of guitar pick: those intended for strumming, those intended for picking, and those that are somewhere in between. The thinner the pick, the less resistance you'll get when strumming the strings, so you might want to start with a very thin (.38mm to .46mm) pick, but buy a couple of 'in-between' picks (.60mm) for when we starting playing melody lines, later in the book.

The electric guitarist

If you have an electric guitar, you'll also need an amplifier and a guitar lead to get a sound out of your instrument.

Here's a step-by-step guide to setting up:

1 Attach your guitar strap. Make sure that the strap is adjusted to a comfortable length. A low-slung guitar looks cool but is actually much more difficult to play – as long as your right and left hands feel comfortable on the guitar your position is probably right.

2 Plug one end of your guitar lead into the socket on your guitar.

3 Take the other end of the lead and plug it into the socket marked 'input' on your amplifier. Make sure that the volume is down on your amplifier before plugging in.

4 Adjust the volume controls on the amplifier and on your guitar until you can hear a sound from the amplifier.

If you can't hear any sound, check that the amp is plugged in and switched on, and that the volume control on your guitar is turned up.

Guitar turned up to 10

Tip

What kind of amp you buy may depend on your relationship with your neighbours! Standard tube and valve guitar amplifiers sound best when played pretty loud and are less effective at a low volume. If playing loud is going to be a problem, you should look for a digital 'solid state' amplifier, which can produce overdriven and distorted tones at a low volume.

Effects pedals

If you're lucky enough to have an effects unit such as a distortion or wah-wah pedal you can have even more fun! Effects pedals (or stomp boxes) take the sound from your guitar and change it before it gets passed on to the amplifier. They can be powered by 9V batteries or by a separate mains adaptor.

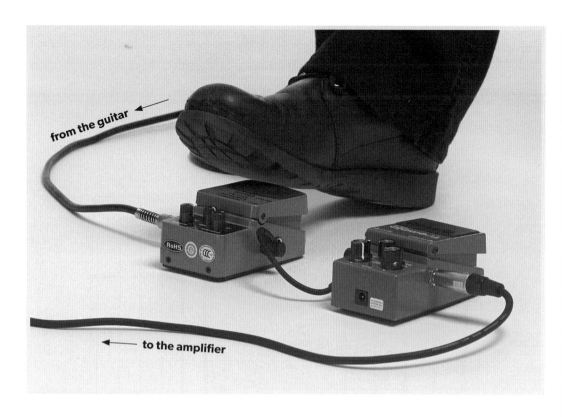

from the guitar

to the amplifier

Take the other end of the lead that is plugged into your guitar and insert it into the input socket on the pedal (sometimes marked 'instrument').

Then take another lead; insert one end of it into the pedal socket marked output (or amplifier) and the other end into the input socket on your amplifier.

Once input and output leads are in, the pedal is activated by stomping on the foot-operated switch.

When the pedal is not switched on you should still be able hear the sound of your guitar as before – the effect is 'bypassed' – but when you step on the switch the sound should change as the effect kicks in.

Pedals can also be 'chained' together to create more original guitar sounds. Contrary to popular opinion, it isn't cheating to use lots of stomp boxes! Many of history's most influential guitarists have used effects to achieve their trademark sound.

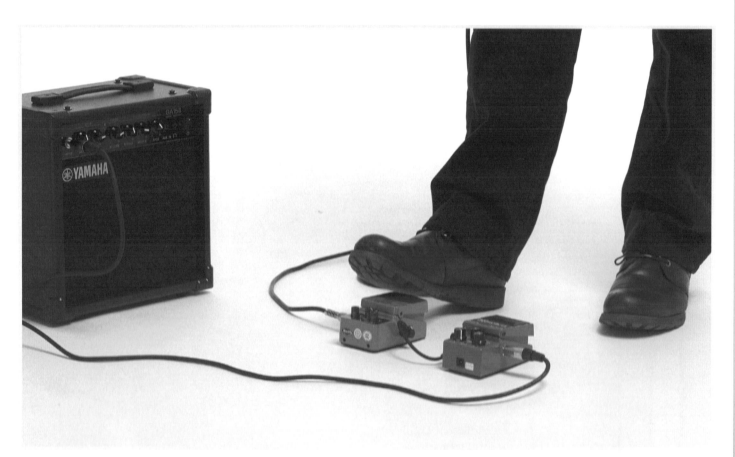

Reading chord boxes

Before we start, it's a good idea to remind ourselves of the basics of guitar notation.

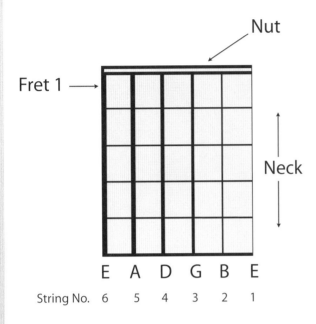

Nut

Fret 1 →

Neck

E A D G B E

String No.   6   5   4   3   2   1

E A D G B E

1st fret

2nd fr.

3rd fr.

4th fr.

5th fr.

Chord boxes are diagrams of the guitar fretboard, viewed face on, with the guitar pointing upwards, as illustrated in the diagrams above.

The horizontal double line at the top is the nut; the horizontal lines below it are the frets.

The vertical lines are the strings starting from the thickest string, E (or 6th) on the left to the thin E or (1st) on the right.

The fingers of your left hand are numbered 1, 2, 3 and 4, with 1 being your index finger – as shown in the diagram, right. Any dots with numbers inside them indicate which finger goes where on the fretboard.

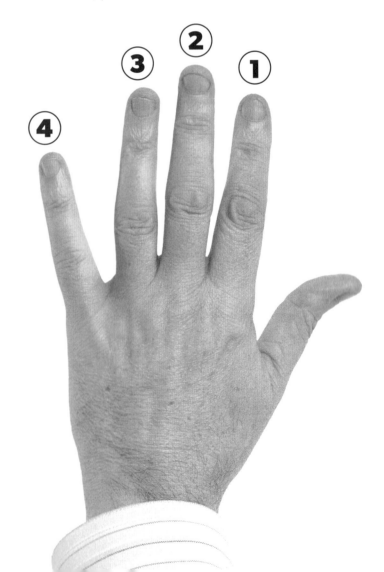

D

X   X   O

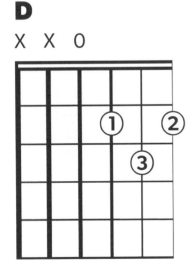

Any strings marked with an **X** must not be played, while an **O** means that the string is played open – with no fingers holding it down.

Be aware that all chords are major chords, unless otherwise stated. Therefore, the chord on the left is described as 'D', but in full is 'D major'.

Reading TAB

Next we're going to look at the basics of guitar tablature, or 'TAB'.

Compared to chord boxes, TAB is a more advanced system of notation, and one that is useful for playing riffs and melodies, which we'll get on to later in the book.

Take a good look at the TAB extract to the right. It's important that you understand which string is which; unlike the chord boxes, TAB doesn't quite represent a guitar the way that it physically appears. It might well seem that the strings are shown in reverse order.

Let's take a look at the notes of the TAB extract above, and see if we can play them on the guitar.

The first note is an **F♯**, played on the 2nd fret of the thinnest E string (string 1)

The next note is a **D**, played on the 3rd fret of the B string (string 2)

The next note is an **A**, played on the 2nd fret of the G string (string 3)

The last note is a **D**, played on the open D string (string 4)

Did you recognise what you just played? It was the D major chord shape, as shown on the previous page. Chords can be presented in either TAB or chord boxes, but boxes are often easier to read, so that's where we'll start.

Three major chords

In this section, we'll be learning three very useful major chords, which together will enable you to play through a whole variety of songs.

E chord

The E major chord is a good place to start, as it uses all the strings on the guitar.

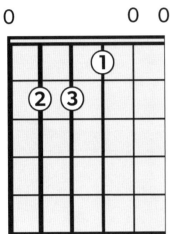

Left hand position

When playing chords, try to keep the left hand relaxed. The left-hand thumb should be roughly vertical behind the neck and roughly behind the 1st and 2nd fingers. Importantly, your fingers should be arched over the fretboard (see the picture above), not lying flat.

If the chord rings out clearly and cleanly – well done, please move on! If it sounds buzzy and 'dead', you should experiment more with your left-hand position. You need to apply quite a bit of pressure on to the fretboard, and your hand needs to be in a position that makes it comfortable to do so. You may also need to cut your nails – long fingernails will prevent you from pushing down properly on to the frets.

Remember that you are calling on muscles that haven't had much use in a while, so initially your hands may get quite tired.

Tip

If the chord still sounds messy, you will need to play each string in the chord individually to isolate the problem note(s).

D Chord

Most players think of D as a triangle shape on the neck. Avoid strumming the sixth and fifth strings, and take note of the fingering. Again, make sure that your left-hand thumb is resting behind the neck of the guitar, and your hand is arched, rather than flat.

X X O

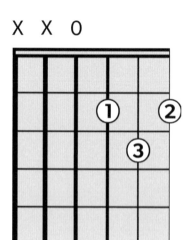

A Chord

For the chord of A, don't strum the (thickest) sixth string. Because this is a more awkward chord, it can be played with a few different fingerings. You might like to try swapping the 1st and 2nd fingers over.

X O   O

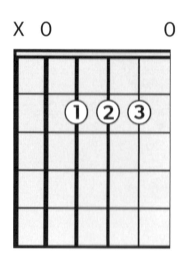

Simple strumming

Now that we've covered the chords of A, D and E, let's do some playing!

To follow are three very simple exercises for you to play through. Don't be put off by the musical notation, as all you need to do is strum one chord in time with the backing track (**Tracks 6 - 8**).
To start with, you will just be using downstrokes ↓ before graduating to upstrokes ↑ at the end of the exercise.

There are four beats in each bar, as marked under the musical stave. At the end of each exercise, upstrokes are played in between the beats – these 'in between' beats are shown under the stave as '&'.

If the musical notation is unclear or unfamiliar, first listen to the backing track on the CD, and then play along with the recording.

Play through the sequence, first using only an **E** chord (**Track 6**).

After that, play through the sequence, using only an **A** chord (**Track 7**)

Finally play through the sequence, using just a **D** chord (**Track 8**)

Tip

Musical terminology
Just so that you know the proper musical terms for what you have been playing, the note lengths have been written on the score. For the first line, you play 'whole notes' (notes which last a whole bar); for the second line, you play **half-notes**, which individually last for half a bar, followed on the third line by **quarter-notes**, which last for a quarter of a bar each, and on the last line by **eighth-notes**, which last for an eighth of a bar.

 6 7 8 Play through the sequence below, using just an **E** chord (**Track 6**), then just an **A** chord (**Track 7**), then just a **D** chord (**Track 8**).

Whole notes

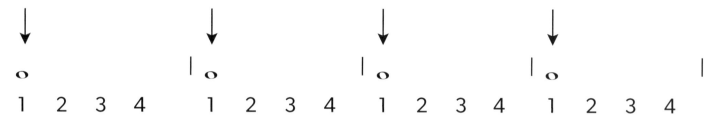

Half-notes

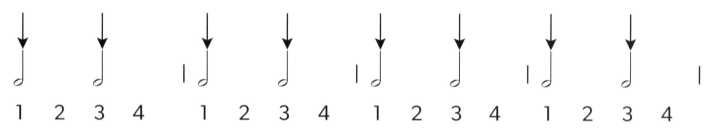

Quarter-notes

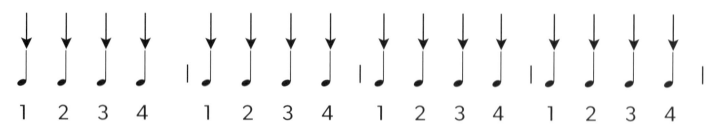

Eighth-notes

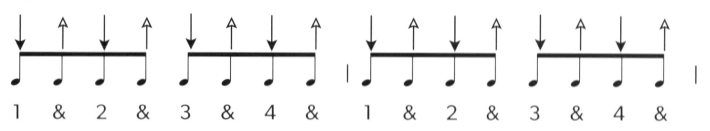

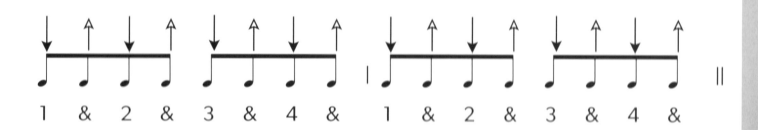

Changing chords

Now it's time to try changing chords from bar to bar. For Track 9 let's use only downstrokes and play one chord per bar.

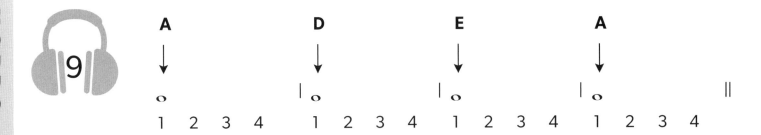

Try playing along with backing **Track 9**. Think ahead and prepare the next shape chord as soon as you've played the previous one.

Now try two strums per chord – i.e. on beats 1 and 2 of each bar. This leaves you the duration of beats 3 and 4 to change to the next shape. Can you feel when to change chord?

Once you've perfected two strums per bar, try moving up to three chords per bar (on beats 1, 2 and 3). This only gives you one beat to change between chord shapes! Play along with **Track 10**.

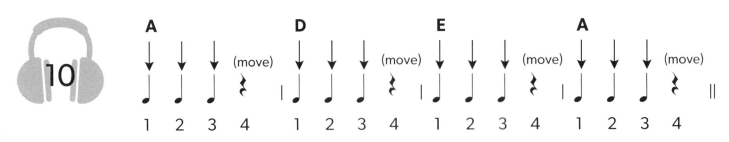

Tip
If you can't change chord fast enough initially, just ignore the strumming and simply move from one chord to the next in your own time until it feels comfortable.

The objective is to make the chord changes as quick and smooth as possible. Try to strum for longer and longer, leaving less and less time for your left hand to change shape. Listen to **Track 11** to hear how this should sound.

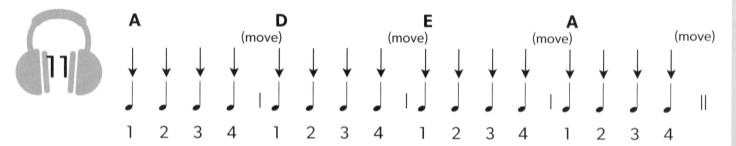

The next step is to play the upstrokes as well.

Eventually, you will be strumming eight times per bar (four up and four down). You may want to start by missing out the final upstroke, using that pause to change chords. Once you feel confident with that, put the final upstroke back in – you'll now have to change shape in between the last upstroke of one bar and the first downstroke of the next one.

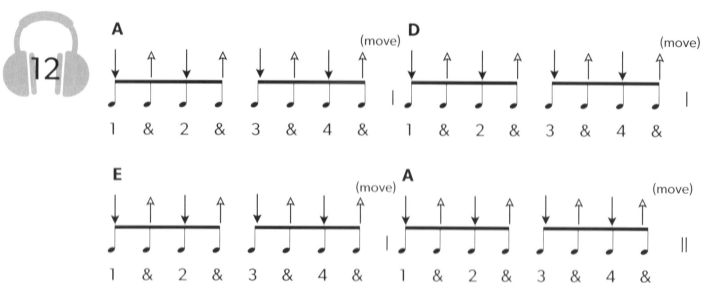

Blue Suede Shoes

Now that you have the chords A, D and E at your fingertips, you should be able to strum through quite a few tunes, especially folk and blues songs.

We're going to start with Elvis Presley's version of Carl Perkins' rock'n'roll standard, 'Blue Suede Shoes'. Carl Perkins' recording is almost identical except for a slightly awkward intro, so you're better off sticking to the Elvis Presley version for now.

To begin with simply play each chord once, where you see its letter name marked in the music (see the next page).

After this, move to this simple strumming pattern, below, playing one chord per bar.

Once you feel confident with this, you can progress to a more advanced strumming pattern used during the chorus. This involves playing downstrokes on every beat, with a quick upstroke at the end of the bar.

The full strumming for the song has been written above the music on the next page.

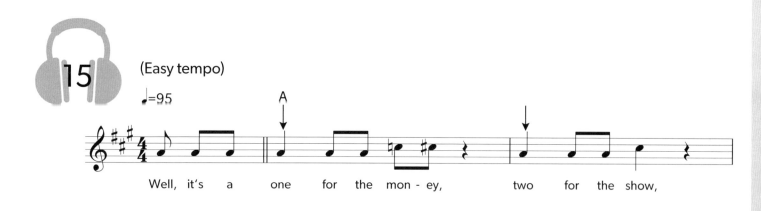

(Easy tempo)

♩=95

Well, it's a   one   for the mon - ey,   two   for   the   show,

three   to   get - a - rea - dy   now   go,   cat,   go.   But   don't___

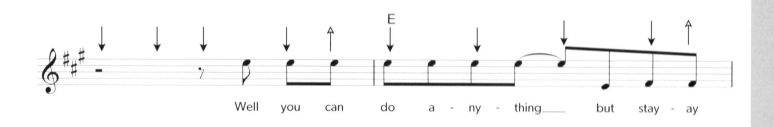

___ you   step   on   my   blue___ suede   shoes.___

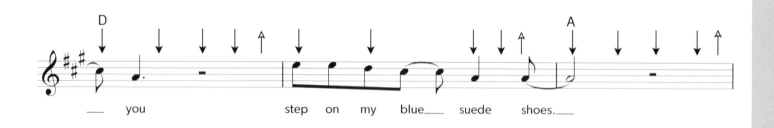

Well   you   can   do   a - ny - thing___   but   stay - ay

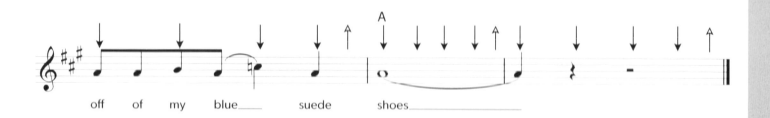

off   of   my   blue___   suede   shoes___

Twist And Shout

Next up is the Beatles' version of the Isley Brothers hit, 'Twist And Shout'. Famously, the song had to be recorded in one take as John Lennon's voice had almost given up after a hard day's recording, resulting in a focused performance from the band, and a larynx-tearing vocal from Lennon.

Start by playing through the song, just strumming each chord once when you see it marked in the music. After that, it shouldn't take long for you to master this simple strumming pattern, which is a mix of down- and upstrokes.

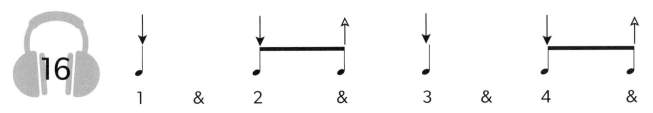

The actual strumming pattern has much more of an emphasis on the upstrokes, creating an exciting, syncopated rhythm. If you're feeling confident with the rhythm above then try the advanced pattern below. You may find it easiest to keep your hand moving up and down on every eighth-note, even if your pick isn't always making contact with the strings. This will create a better flow and groove to your strumming.

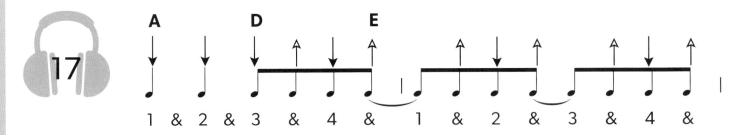

Using a capo

The recording of this song is in a different key to what you see written – the relationships between the chords are the same, but the recording starts on an A chord, not an E chord. To get around this, we need to use a capo.

Capos are used by guitarists who need to raise or lower the key of the song, usually to fit a singer's vocal range. In this case, we're going to raise the pitch of the chords by placing the capo on the 5th fret. If your capo is adjustable, make sure that is clamped (not too tightly) around the guitar neck. Once it is attached, you should treat the capo as the nut of the guitar.

It's important to note that this song will still work without a capo – it only becomes essential if you want to play along with the recording.

18

♩=127

Simple strumming:

I Fought The Law

'I Fought The Law' has a fascinating history: written by a former member of Buddy Holly's band, the Crickets, and then made famous by another tragic Texan rock 'n' roll star, Bobby Fuller, the song was then covered in 1979 by The Clash, who transformed it into a punk anthem. We'll be looking at the version recorded by The Clash.

Strumming

The strumming pattern to this song isn't entirely consistent, and often follows the vocal melody, so before starting, it's a good idea to listen to both The Clash's recording as well as the audio provided with this book.

For the majority of the song, the guitar plays the following pattern:

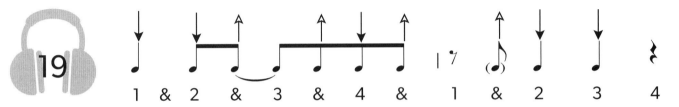

You'll hear that there are two versions of this pattern: one including a D chord and one including an E chord. If you find the upbeat in bar 2 of each pattern too challenging, please leave it out.

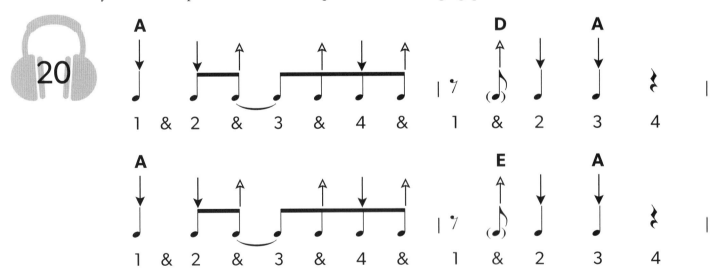

When we move to the bridge section, the strumming pattern becomes a bit more consistent, just repeating the first bar of the pattern we've already learnt.

Capo

When playing along with the recording, you'll need to place a capo at the 5th fret.

Tip

Which capo?

The easiest capos to use are spring-loaded 'trigger' capos, while the more expensive Shubb capos work like a traditional clamp, where the pressure of the capo can be adjusted. There are also cheap capos available that tie around the neck using a fabric strap – however, these are quite flimsy and definitely the least reliable option!

♩=154

Break-ing rocks_ in the hot sun I fought the law and the, the law won.
Rob-bing peo-ple with a six gun. I fought the law and the, the law won.

I fought the law and the, the law won. I need-ed mo-ney 'cause I had none.
I fought the law and the, the law won. I lost me girl_ and I lost me fun.

I fought the law and the, the law won. I fought the law and the,

(Bridge)

the law won. I left my ba-by and it feels so bad. I guess my race is run.

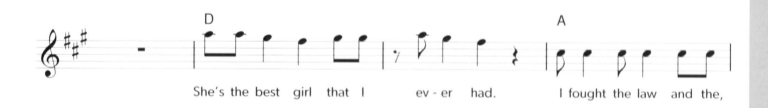

She's the best girl that I ev-er had. I fought the law and the,

the law won. I fought the law and the...

Words & Music by Sonny Curtis

New chord shapes

With three songs down, it's definitely time to refresh your chord repertoire. So far we've only looked at major chords, but in this chapter, we'll be mixing them together with minor chords, and also chords known as '7' chords.

Minor chords

Take a look at A minor, which you'll notice is marked as 'Am'. The lower case 'm' refers to 'minor'.

A minor

23

You should also notice that the A minor chord has a different flavour to its major counterpart; you may recognise it as the opening chord in a number of mournful ballads, including The Rolling Stones' 'Angie' and Radiohead's 'Street Spirit (Fade Out)'.

Play the chord of A minor, again checking each string individually to make sure that it is ringing out clearly. You may well find that this chord is easier to play than A major, as the fingers are not so cramped together.

D minor

24

Any major chord will have a minor counterpart – let's look at D minor …

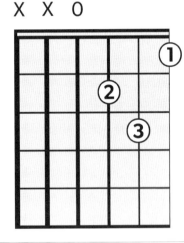

E minor

25

… and E minor.

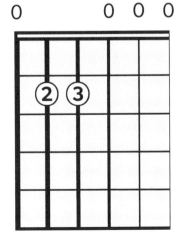

7 Chords

'7' chords are essentially a more sophisticated version of a standard major chord; there is an extra note added: the 7th note of the relevant scale. Although '7' chords originate from classical harmony, they are used extensively in jazz and blues music, and are often used to add a blues-y flavour to a song.

This is particularly noticeable in the verse of 'Mrs. Robinson' (page 35), which uses the chords E7 and A7. You'll find the D7 chord used a lot in the song 'Blanket On The Ground', on page 32.

Again, any major chord will have a '7' counterpart.

E7

26

This E7 chord is the same as a regular E chord, but with the 3rd finger removed.

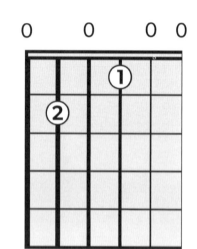

A7

27

Please note that this fingering for the A7 chord is an easier beginners fingering. You can try playing this chord with fingers 2 and 3 instead.

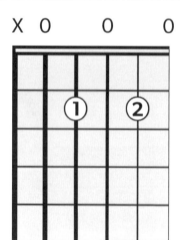

D7

28

This D7 chord is the same shape as a D chord, but upside down.

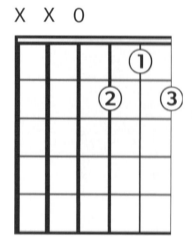

Jolene

Country star Dolly Parton's hit single 'Jolene' has been covered by everyone from Olivia Newton-John to the White Stripes. It's a testament to Dolly's songwriting that 'Jolene' is still a firm favourite, despite being first released in 1973.

We're going to start this chapter with another three-chord song, but this time the chords will be: A minor, C and G. We've just looked at A minor, but C (major) and G (major) may well be new to you.

C major

There are a couple of different ways of playing a G chord. This is probably the easiest fingering for a G chord, but feel free to use any alternative fingerings that you might already know.

Capo

If you're playing along with the original recording of this song, you'll need to place a capo at the 4th fret.

G major

Which strings to strum?

When strumming, you don't have to strum every single string that belongs to the chord – here, you can create much more effective groove by strumming just the lowest note of the chord on beats 1 and 2 (which have been marked * in the notation), and then playing the full chord on all of the other strums. If you are playing at a faster tempo, you may find it easier to leave out the upstroke.

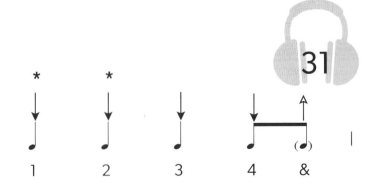

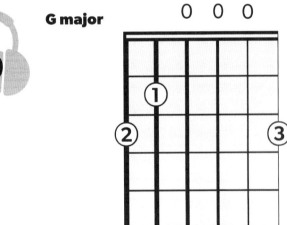

*   *

1   2   3   4   &

Words & Music by Dolly Parton
© 1973 VELVET APPLE MUSIC - All Rights Reserved - Used by Permission of Carlin Music Corp., London, NW1 8BD - for the WORLD excluding Scandinavia, Australia and New Zealand, Japan, South Africa, Canada and the United States of America.

Blanket On The Ground

This classic country-pop song, released by Billie Jo Spears in 1975 is a great song to help you hone your country-style strumming.

Strumming

There are two obvious challenges to the strumming pattern in this song: firstly, the song is played at quite a fast tempo, and secondly the rhythm of the guitar is 'swung'. This only really affects the penultimate chord of the strumming pattern (the upstroke), which is played extremely clipped and short.

As with the strumming pattern to 'Jolene', you shouldn't play every string of the chord all the time. The majority of the strumming pattern alternates between the bass (lowest) note of the chord, and then strumming the whole chord. You'll also see that it uses mainly downstrokes.

Remember to alternate between playing the bass note of the chord, and strumming the whole chord.

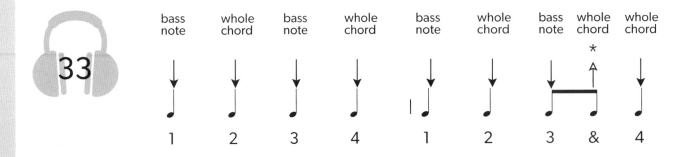

(* upstroke not played on repeat)

'7' chords

You'll see that there are a couple of '7' chords used in the song – the shapes for these are shown on page 27.

Capo

If you're playing along with the recording of this song, you'll have to place your capo on the 3rd fret.

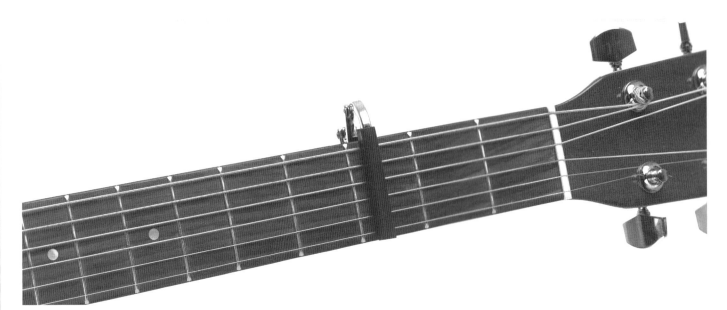

Words & Music by Roger Bowling
© Copyright 1975 Brougham-Hall-Music Co Inc.
Sony/ATV Music Publishing.
All Rights Reserved. International Copyright Secured.

Like A Rolling Stone

Heralding Bob Dylan's transition from folk to rock music, 'Like A Rolling Stone' was released in 1965, the first single from his landmark album, *Highway 61 Revisited*.

This song includes only one completely new chord – the chord of F major. It has a few different fingerings, some of which are quite advanced, and for that reason, we're going to look at two options for playing the chord. Our first option is a simplified chord, called F major 7. It's a more complicated name, but a much easier fingering.

F maj 7

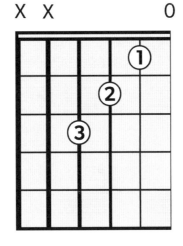

F

Your alternative is to play a slightly more advanced version of an F chord. It involves a 'barre', where your first finger is held across the thinnest two strings. You will need to apply a bit more pressure to get the note on the thinnest string to ring out; 'digging' your thumb into the back of the neck may help with this.

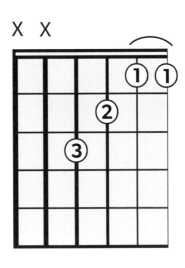

As this song is taken from Dylan's 'electric' period, you can strum quite forcefully – don't be afraid to play good and loud. The strumming pattern below is quite basic, so you may also want to add some extra upstrokes to the rhythm. Please note that for most of this song you will be playing two chords per bar, changing chords on beat 3.

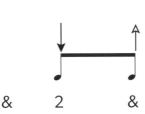

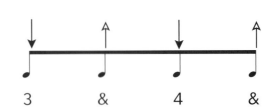

1 & 2 & 3 & 4 &

Mrs. Robinson

Written for the film *The Graduate*, Simon & Garfunkel's 'Mrs. Robinson' was one of the duo's biggest hits, topping the US charts in 1968.

Like many of Simon & Garfunkel's songs, 'Mrs. Robinson' is a very satisfying song to play on the acoustic guitar; it uses a mixture of open chords and a very recognisable acoustic guitar riff.

The rhythm pattern evolves slightly throughout the song, but its basis is this pattern below; feel free to add in extra strums as you wish.

The song also includes a very memorable riff, which may take a little while to fully master, and require practising slowly at first. The crucial thing to remember is that the riff starts just after the first beat of the bar. To help you, the 'count' has been written above the bar – you'll see that the riff starts on the '&' after beat 1.

The next challenge is to play a hammer-on (there is more information on hammer-ons on page 53), between the second and third notes.

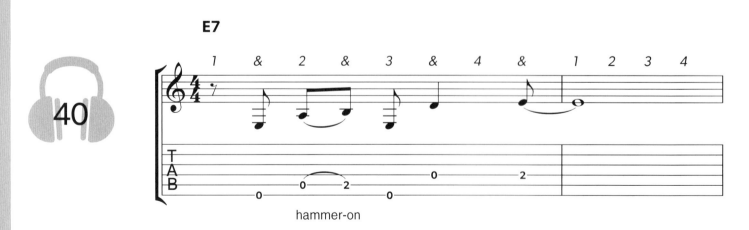

hammer-on

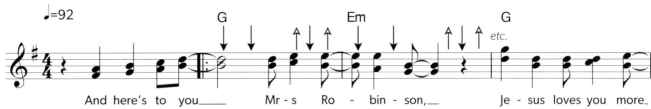

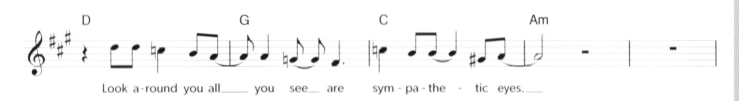

Power chords

Power chords are an essential part of any rock guitarist's repertoire – they appear in rock music throughout the ages, and fortunately for us, they consist of just three notes. Power chords are denoted with a '5' after the chord name.

F5

42

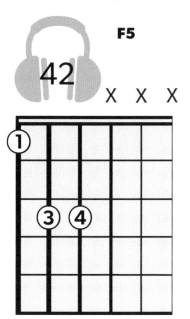

G5

43

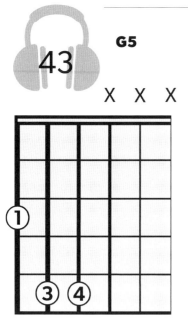

Notice that these power chords use exactly the same shape. To move from one power chord to the next, slide up or down the fretboard, making sure you release the pressure in your hand while you slide, and then push your fingers back down on to the fretboard to play the next chord.

Because we're playing just the lowest three strings, you need to ensure that the thinnest three strings are muted. Lightly rest your first finger against the thinnest three strings, as shown above – this will prevent them from ringing out.

Tip
Muting the top three strings becomes even more important if you're using distortion and/or playing with your amp turned up loud.

Root notes

The lowest note in a chord is known as the 'root note'. It is the root note of a chord that gives it its name – the lowest note in a **C** chord is a **C**, the lowest note in a **G** power chord is a **G**, and so on.

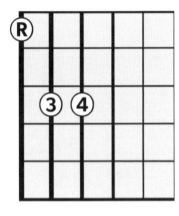

We've seen how power chords all use the same shape – by sliding the shape up the neck of the guitar, you can play 12 different power chords. All we need to know now is which power chord is played at which fret.

Look at the diagram to the right – all of the notes on the thickest string have been written out. It's these notes, which you'll play with your 1st finger, that determine which power chord you are playing.

Start by playing the F5 power chord. Your 1st finger should be holding down the note on the 1st fret of the thickest string – as you'll see from the diagram, that note is F. Slide the shape up two frets to play the G5 power chord, or a further four frets to play a B5 power chord.

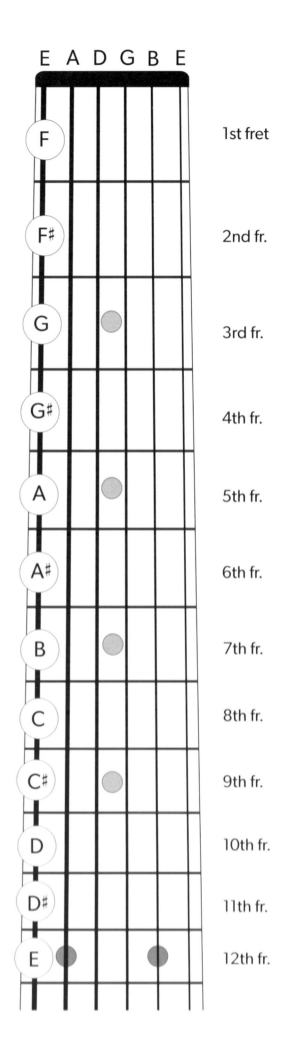

You Really Got Me

The Kinks' first hit from 1964 has a surprisingly hard rock edge to it, thanks to a biting, overdriven guitar sound and a memorable power chord riff.

Riffs

This song can be reduced to three separate riffs, all of which use power chords, as well as the same rhythm and strumming pattern.
Here is the first riff:

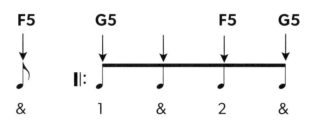

You'll see on the next page that the second riff is identical, except that it now moves between a G5 and an A5.

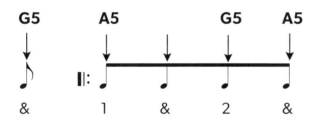
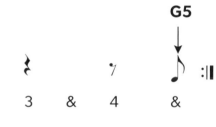

The riff for the chorus is also identical, except that we move between a C5 and D5, both of which are high up the fretboard.

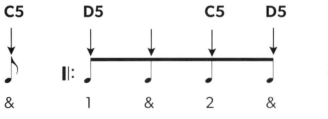

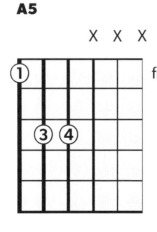
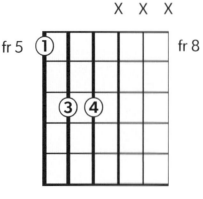
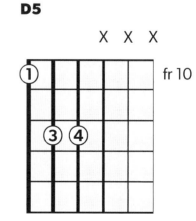

♩=138

Girl you real - ly got me go - ing, you got me

so I don't know what I'm do - in'.

Yeah, you real - ly got me now, you got me

so I can't sleep at night.

Yeah, you real - ly got me now, you got me

so I don't know what I'm do - in' oh. Oh,

yeah, you real - ly got me now, you got me

so I can't sleep at night, you real - ly got me, you

real - ly got me, you real - ly got me.

Words & Music by Ray Davies
© Copyright 1964 Edward Kassner Music Company Limited.
All Rights Reserved. International Copyright Secured.

Wild World

Cat Stevens' 'Wild World' (1970) uses a more complex chord sequence, interspersed with a few melody lines or 'runs', based on a C major scale. Let's start by looking at the new chords:

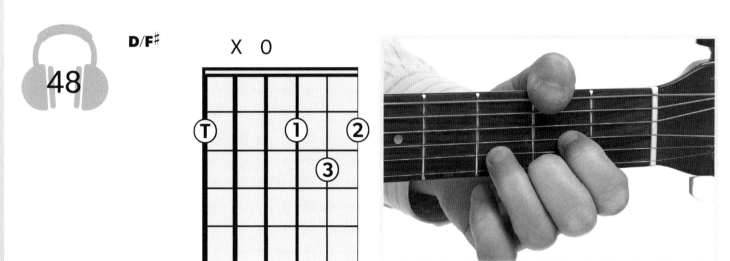

This chord is a 'slash' chord, meaning the first letter, **D**, is the overall chord, however the bass note is the letter after the chord – in this case, **F♯**. So we are playing a D chord with an F♯ in the bass.

This is also the first time that you've needed to use your fretting-hand thumb; you may have to shift your hand position slightly to get it in place. This 'slash' chord is essentially a D chord, but with an F♯ played by the thumb. If using your thumb is too challenging, please play a standard D chord instead.

We then have an F chord; either the Fmaj7 or the more advanced F chord that we learnt on page 32 will work here.

The only other new chord is a Cmaj7. Major 7 chords have a slightly jazzier sound, due to a harmonic 'clash' within the chord. This chord is very easy to play – the fingering is the same as that for a standard C chord, but without the first finger, so the open B string is allowed to ring out.

Let's have a look at the song itself; after that we'll investigate some of the melody lines used in the song. The strumming pattern for this song (**Track 50**) is written above the music on the next page. Remember that when strumming you don't have to play the whole chord all the time – sometimes just playing the bass note is enough.

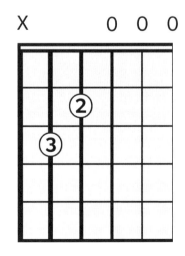

50 51

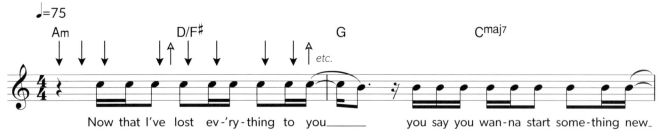

Now that I've lost ev-'ry-thing to you___ you say you wan-na start some-thing new___

___ and it's break-ing my heart_ you're leav - ing. Ba - by I'm griev - in'!

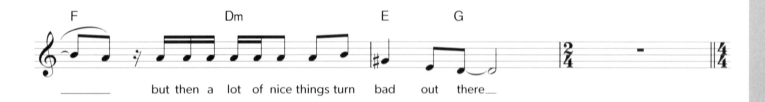

But if you want to leave take good care, hope you have a lot of nice things to wear_

___ but then a lot of nice things turn bad out there___

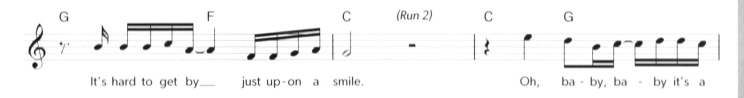

Oh ba - by, ba - by it's a wild world.

It's hard to get by___ just up-on a smile. Oh, ba - by, ba - by it's a

wild world. I'll al-ways re - mem - ber you___ like a child, girl.___

Major scales and runs

The chorus to 'Wild World' uses two riffs, both of which use notes from the C major scale.

They are marked in the music (on the previous page) as Run 1 and Run 2.
Pick both patterns using 'alternate-picking'; alternate between down- and up-picks, starting with a down-pick.

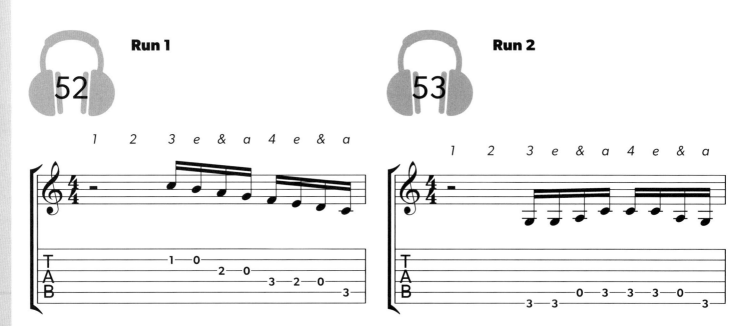

It's fairly common to insert 'runs' into chord sequences, particularly at a point where there is a break in the vocal melody.

Below is the scale of C major – play through the notes slowly, up and down, with a metronome if possible.

C major scale

Once you are familiar with the notes of the scale, you might like to insert similar 'runs' into some of the songs that we've already learnt, which are also in C major.

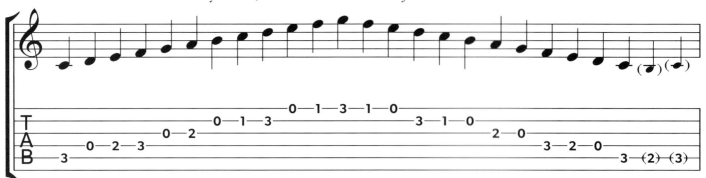

You'll find that this scale works well with 'Like A Rolling Stone', the chorus for 'Wild World' and 'Jolene' (for the latter, remember that you'll need a capo at the 4th fret if you're playing along with the recording). You'll hear and see that two extra notes have been added at the end of the scale – this is just to make it flow better when you are performing it.

If you're creating your own runs, start simply. You might even want to take one of the runs from 'Wild World' and adapt it slightly, changing the notes, or the rhythm, like so.

Run 1 (altered)   **Run 2 (altered)**

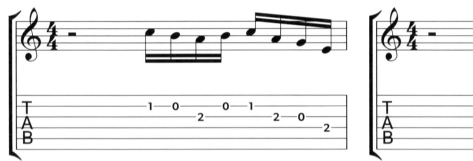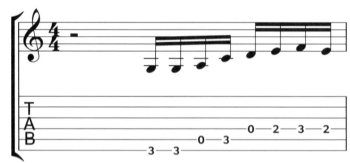

Just so that you have more than one scale in your locker, here is a G major scale. It's a very useful scale, as G major is a very common key. You'll find that this scale works well for creating solos and runs over the chorus of Mrs. Robinson, for example.

 **G major scale**

You'll hear and see that the the top G is played twice – this is just to make the scale flow better when you are performing it.

Playing arpeggio style

So far we have only strummed through songs. Strumming is a fundamental guitar technique, but not always the most subtle!

In this lesson, we're going to use chords that we've already learnt, but this time we will pick out individual notes of the chord, rather than strum them all in one 'block'. This can be referred to as playing 'arpeggio style'.

Although you can use a plectrum to do this, you'll achieve a characteristically folky style if you use your fingers to pick the notes. While classical guitarists tend to pick using their fingernails, it is common for folk or pop players to use the fleshy 'pad' at the tip of their fingers. So that you know which finger to use, we're going to label them: **T 1 2 3 4**.

Let's start by playing an A minor chord, arpeggio style. Try not to think about your fretting hand at all – make an A minor chord and keep it there, on the fretboard.

56 Play this A minor chord through a few times, with a metronome if possible, starting slowly and getting faster.

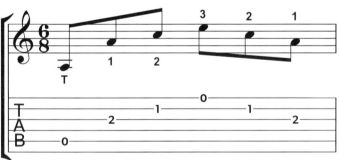

57 Now try this very similar pattern, on a C major chord:

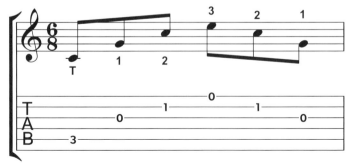

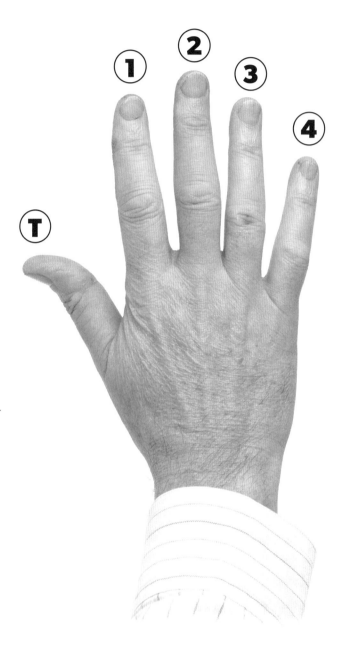

Now try moving from the A minor chord to the C major chord. Practise this as slowly as you need to, making sure that you can eventually play both chords in succession, without pausing in the middle.

House Of The Rising Sun

Your next task is to play through an arrangement of 'House Of The Rising Sun'. The arrangement is written in TAB, but hopefully you will notice that the fretting hand simply holds down familiar chord shapes. You may notice that there are now six beats in each bar, as the song is in 6/8 time, a common time signature for ballads.

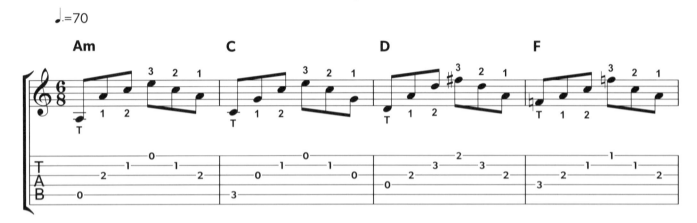

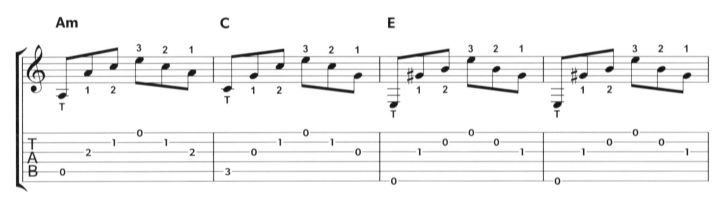

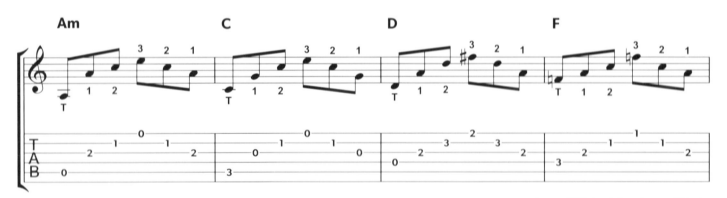

Mad World

For our next arpeggio style song, we're going to look at an arrangement of 'Mad World', using the version by Gary Jules and Michael Andrews as our template.

Please be aware that you'll need to place a capo on the first fret of your guitar if you want to play along with the recording.

Verse chord sequence

Practise the verse chord sequence slowly. Again, we're using chord shapes that we've already learnt, so you should be concentrating most on your picking hand.

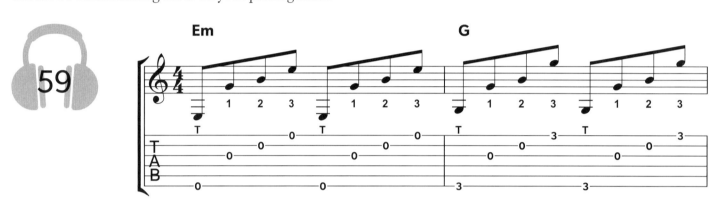

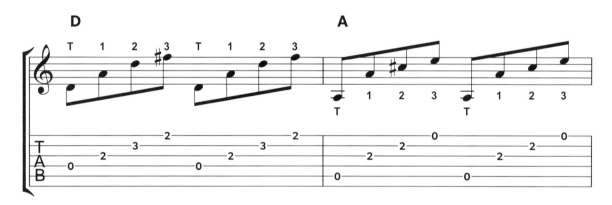

The chorus chord sequence is even simpler – it just repeats the Em and A chords from the verse sequence.

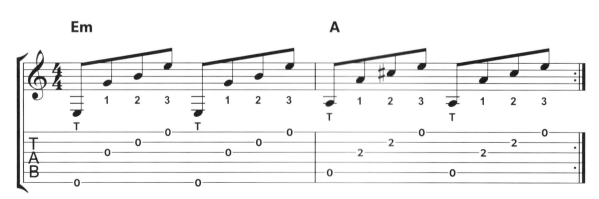

♩=86

Em
1. All a-round me are fa - mi - liar fa - ces, worn out pla - ces,
2. Child-ren wait-ing for the day they feel_ good, hap - py birth - day,

A **Em** **G** **D**
worn out fa - ces.____ Bright and ear - ly for their dai-ly ra - ces, go-ing no - where,
hap - py birth - day.____ And I feel the way that ev-'ry child_should, sit and lis - ten,

A **Em** **G**
go - ing no - where.____ Their tears are fill - ing up their glass - es,
sit and lis - ten.____ Went to school and I was ver - y ner - vous,

D **A** **Em**
no ex - pres - sion, no ex - pres - sion.____ Hide my head, I wan - na
no one knew_ me, no one knew_ me.____ Hel - lo teach-er, tell me

G **D** **A**
drown my sor - row, no to - mor - row, no to - mor - row.____
what's my les - son? Look right through me, look right through me.____

Em **A** **Em**
And I find it kind - a fun - ny, I find it kind - a sad, that dreams in which I'm

A **Em** **A** **Em**
dy-ing are the best I've ev-er had. I find it hard to tell you, I find it hard to take, when peo-ple run in

A **Em** **A** **Em** **A**
cir-cles it's a ve-ry, ve-ry mad world.____ Mad world.____

Words & Music by Roland Orzabal

47

Hallelujah

Leonard Cohen's ballad lends itself perfectly to an 'arpeggio-style' interpretation. It has a flowing, 6/8 rhythm and only uses chords that we've already learnt.

Run

In the popular Jeff Buckley arrangement of the song, you'll hear a very simple 'run', connecting the C chord to the A minor chord.

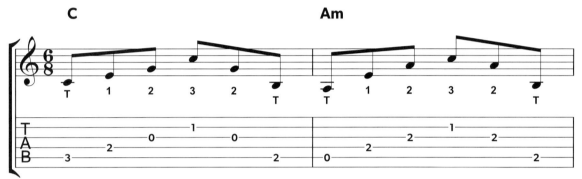

Although the chords may change, your right hand (picking hand) can follow a similar pattern throughout the song. Once you've learnt the song in this arrangement, you could also try creating your own picking patterns, playing the same notes, but in a different order.

Below is an alternative way of playing the opening two chords.

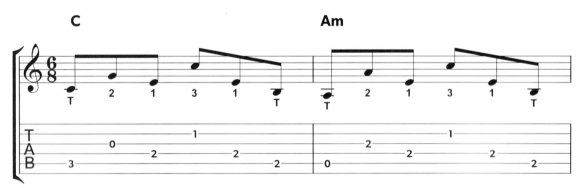

Hopefully there is only one tricky moment in the song, during the lyric 'It goes like the this, the fourth, the fifth'. Here we have three chords in quick succession. Below is a suggested way of picking this section.

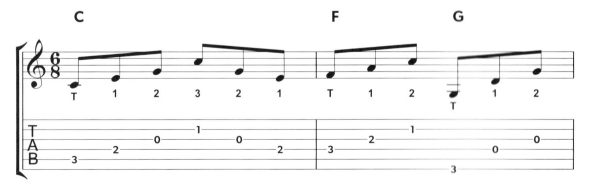

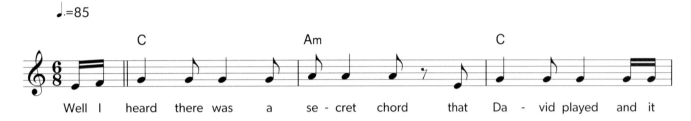

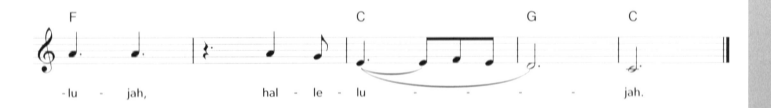

Words & Music by Leonard Cohen
© Copyright 1984 Bad Monk Publishing.
Sony/ATV Music Publishing.
All Rights Reserved. International Copyright Secured.

The pentatonic scale

The pentatonic scale has long been a favourite with guitarists. It's easy to learn, with uncomplicated fingering, and as long as you match up the song to the correct version of the scale, it will sound good no matter what you play.

We're going to start with position 1 of the minor pentatonic, shown below. Don't worry too much about the terminology – 'pentatonic' refers to the fact that there are five different notes in the scale, while the 'minor' label refers to the fact that the first two notes, A–C are a minor interval (they are found in an A minor chord, for example).

A minor pentatonic

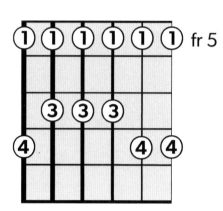

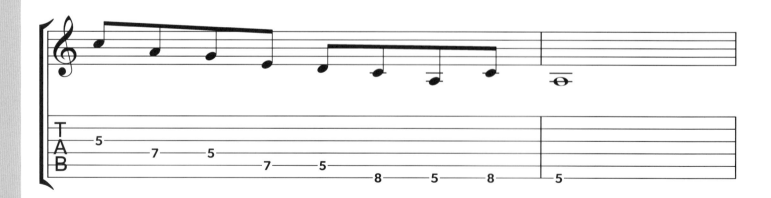

This well-used and hugely versatile scale is the saviour of many a rock soloist. It's most important that you learn the shape of this scale, rather than the individual fret numbers. As with power chords, you can slide this shape up and down the fretboard as you please.

Try playing the same pattern, but up three frets (starting on fret 8). Congratulations! You've just played a C minor pentatonic scale!

Pentatonic riffs

Just because the pentatonic scale is relatively simple, don't think that the professional players never use it.

Eric Clapton's 'Layla' riff uses the D minor pentatonic. David Gilmour's epic solo in Pink Floyd's 'Comfortably Numb' features runs taken from the B minor pentatonic scale. Below are two further well-known, and slightly easier examples.

I Shot The Sheriff

Each chorus to Bob Marley's 'I Shot The Sheriff' is preceded by a riff based on the G minor pentatonic scale. To play the scale in its entirety, use the same pattern that we learnt for the A minor, but shift it down two frets, so that you start on fret 3.

♩=194

(Gm)

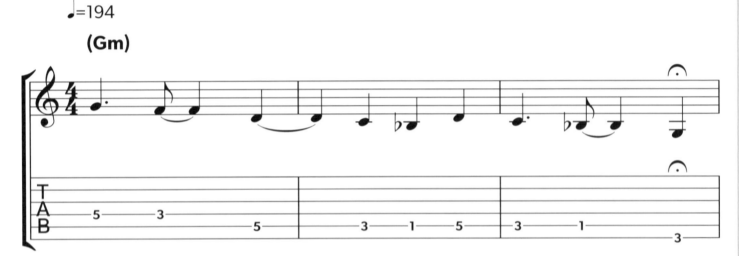

Black Night

This classic Deep Purple riff uses the E minor pentatonic scale. The riff is played using a 'swing' rhythm, whereby the eighth-notes follow a long/short pattern. Listen to and copy the rhythm of the recording.

♩=134

(Em)

The blues scale

Once you're familiar with the minor pentatonic scale, you're one small step away from playing the blues scale, another extremely useful pattern of notes, beloved of many blues and 'classic rock' guitarists such as Jimi Hendrix, B.B. King, Chuck Berry and Eric Clapton.

The blues scale includes one extra note – often referred to as the '**blue note**' – which is crucial to giving the scale its distinctive, 'bluesy' character.

A blues scale

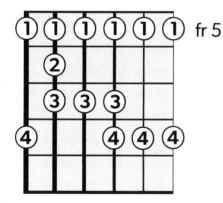

Have you spotted the extra note? It's the $E^\flat$, in between the notes D and E. Practise the scale, slowly at first. Now play through the scale again, but pause on either of the $E^\flat$ notes; hopefully you'll notice how this note stands out compared to the other notes in the scale.

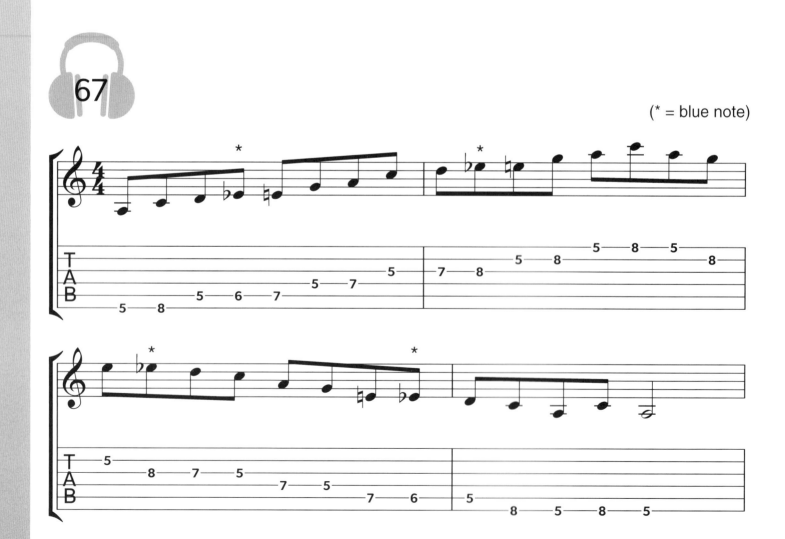

(* = blue note)

Blues solos

You can now use the notes of the blues scale to make up some short solos. The solos below use notes from the A blues scale.

Notice that the solo includes a slide – this is easier to achieve than you might imagine; simply play the first note of the slide, and without re-picking the string, slide your fretting-hand finger up the fretboard from

fret 7 to fret 9. You'll play two notes, but pluck the string once. The next slide reverses this action, and you'll slide down from fret 9 to fret 7.

Hammer-ons

Playing a hammer-on follows the same principle as playing a slide – you play two notes, but only pick the string once. It's also sometimes called a 'slur'. Let's start with this very simple hammer-on. Pick an open G string, and then bring your 2nd finger sharply down on to the second fret.

Now try playing the solo below. It's the same as the solo that you've just played, except that it has been adapted to include three hammer-ons. Practise it slowly, remembering that for each hammer-on you will play two notes but pick only once.

* = hammer-on

53

Sunshine Of Your Love

One of the most famous riffs based on the blues scale is the opening riff from 'Sunshine Of Your Love' by Cream (featuring Eric Clapton on guitar).

We can divide the guitar part for the song into two riffs (played during the verse) and three simple chords, played during the chorus.

The first riff uses the notes of the D blues scale. It's played in quite an unusual position, starting right up on the 12th fret of the D string.

Riff 1

(D)

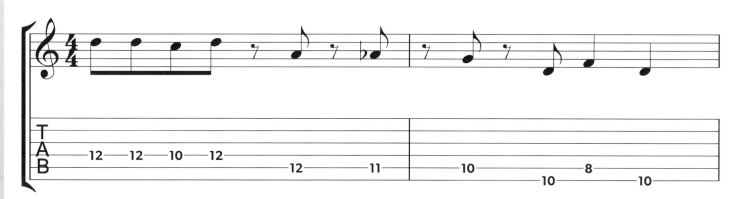

The second riff uses the notes of a G blues scale – it's very similar to the previous riff, but notice that it starts with a small power chord.

Riff 2

(G)

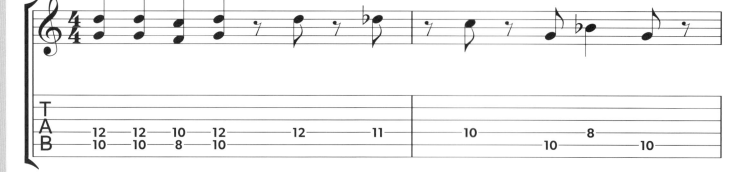

The Chorus uses three chords: A, C and G. To create a more convincing, 'rock' sound, try playing these as power chords.

Turn back to page 37 if you need a reminder on how to play the A, C and G power chords.

73

♩=132

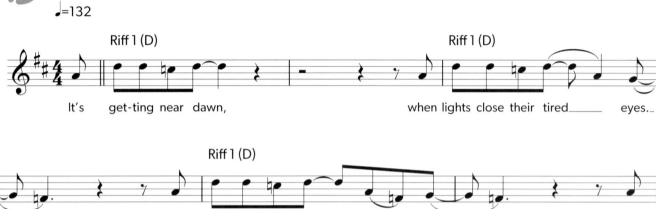

Riff 1 (D)   Riff 1 (D)

It's get-ting near dawn,   when lights close their tired_____ eyes.__

Riff 1 (D)

_____ I'll soon be with you,__ my__ love,_____ to

Riff 1 (D)   Riff 2 (G)

give you my dawn_ sur - prise._____   I'll be with you, dar - ling, soon,_

Riff 2 (G)

_____ I'll be with you when_ the stars____ start__ fall - ing.

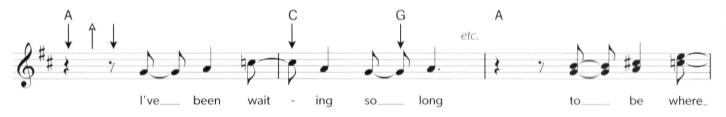

Riff 1 (D)   Riff 1 (D)

A   C   G   A   etc.

I've__ been wait - ing so__ long   to__ be where_

C   G   A   C   G

__ I'm go - ing   in__ the sun - shine of__ your

A

love._____

String bending

String bending is one of those special techniques which distinguish the guitar from many other instruments; it allows you to subtly (or dramatically!) alter the pitch of a note, and to emulate the bends and less rigid pitch of the human voice. It is particularly useful in blues music, where pitch-bending is a defining characteristic of the style.

There are a few basic concepts to remember when bending the strings. Here are some tips to help you get it right:

Hand in position

Bend in action

Support the bending finger
Ideally, you should bend with your 3rd finger – this way you will have both your 2nd and 1st fingers behind it to support it. This will help to stabilise your hand and give it strength. Don't bend with your 1st finger, as it will not be supported, and do not bend using your little finger – it won't be strong enough.

Bend towards you
When bending, your fingers should be pressed down on the fretboard, but moving upwards – towards you.

Use an electric guitar with light-gauge strings
Although string-bending is possible on an acoustic guitar, it isn't advisable for a beginner. Likewise, your strings don't have be light-gauge, but you will find bending much easier if they are.

Bend from your hand
Make sure that your hand is driving the movement of the bend; it should pivot upwards towards you.

Listen to your tuning

The whole point of string-bending is that you are bypassing the rigid tuning that your guitar's fretboard imposes. For now, we're just going to look at bending up one semitone (the equivalent of one fret) or one tone (the equivalent of two frets).

Semitone bend

Tone bend

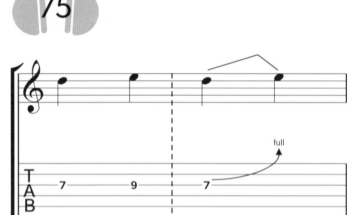

String-bending in context

Try this string-bending example, taken from Noel Gallagher's solo in 'Don't Look Back In Anger'. At its original speed it will be very challenging, so play along with the recording provided, which is at a much more comfortable tempo.

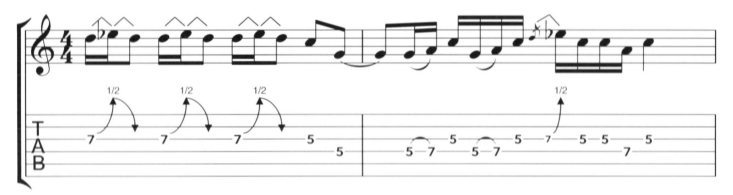

This is as far we're going with your guitar playing; hopefully you've come along way since you restarted! In the next section you'll find some general tips and tricks on how to maintain your instrument.

Revive your guitar

It's possible that your guitar has been unused for quite a while, and possibly gathering dust in a loft or spare bedroom. Well, now's the time to administer some much-needed TLC!

The most important thing to do is to change the strings, which we'll come to on page 60. Before that, we've got some cleaning up to do.

First off, you'll want to dust off the guitar, using a dust cloth. You may want to go even further, using a damp wash cloth to pick off any dirt or grime on the guitar. It's possible that the fretboard will be particularly grimy, in which case you should either loosen the strings or take them off completely, so that you have room to wipe down the fretboard. Some players like to use alcohol swabs to get the dirt off even more effectively.

Once the guitar is clean, a bit of polish will get it looking nice and shiny. If you're using any liquid at all, keep it away from the electrics of the guitar.

Once you are certain that the guitar fretboard is clean, you can condition it using lemon oil. In order to do this, you're best off removing all of the strings, so that you can thoroughly rub the oil into the wood of the fretboard (using a clean cloth).

In order to properly clean the fretboard, you may need to take the strings off completely.

Obviously, there is a limit to the amount of DIY you can safely perform on your guitar. There are many books and websites dedicated to guitar maintenance, but unless you're feeling exceptionally confident, you should probably leave any tampering with the electrics of the guitar, or changing the action, to the professionals.

Pickups can be repaired or replaced, although you may want to leave this to the professionals.

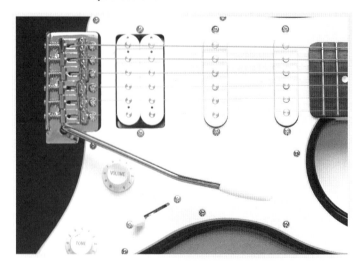

Pick rescue!

One of the most frustrating hazards of playing the acoustic guitar is losing your pick inside the soundhole of the guitar – especially if you don't have a spare! To save you hours of shaking your precious guitar around to retrieve it, simply attach a 'blob' of Blu-tack to the end of pencil and insert it into the soundhole of your guitar. With a bit of manoeuvring, the Blu-tack should grip the pick, allowing you to reclaim it quite easily.

Finally, please remember to store your guitar in a safe place – ideally in a case, and certainly away from radiators or environments where it will experience more extreme temperatures.

Changing strings

There is nothing quite like the tone of new strings on your guitar, but that sound will soon fade. Strings are made from an alloy and therefore tarnish easily, losing tone.

To extend their life always wipe down the instrument at the end of each playing session, taking special care with the strings. A clean dry linen or silk cloth wiped over the strings will remove dirt and moisture.

Strings vary in thickness from the bottom (thickest) to the top (thinnest). The bottom three are wound to give the sound more depth; the top three are just unwound alloy wire. When it's time to change your strings always check you have the right gauges.

The diameter of a string – its gauge – is measured in inches or centimetres: the lower the number, the thinner the string. A set of light gauge strings (0.09-0.42) may be preferable for electric guitar because it makes string-bending easier. A classical or Spanish guitar is intended to have nylon strings, in contrast to its steel-strung relative, the folk acoustic guitar.

Left: Medium gauge strings (acoustic guitar)
Below: Medium gauge strings (electric guitar

1 Removing the old string

First of all, wind down the string that needs replacing, until it is completely slack. Having done this, if you tug on the string, you should be able to remove it completely from the tuning peg.

You now need to detach the string from the base of the guitar. This procedure depends on whether you are restringing an acoustic or an electric guitar.

On an electric guitar, push the string down, through the plate screwed to the back of the guitar. The string should pop through its hole in this back plate. When the string is removed, insert the new string in the same hole, ensuring that the circular stopper is the last thing to go through.

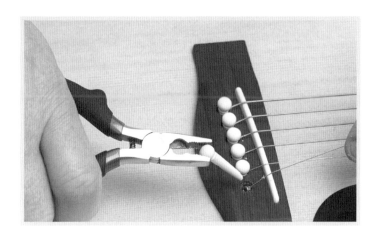

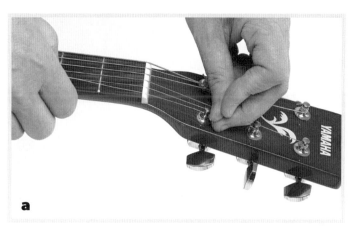

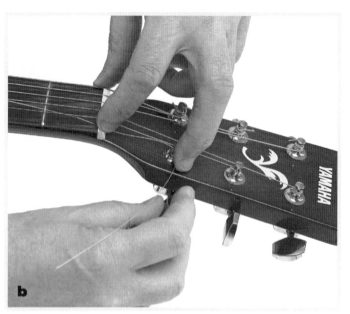

On an acoustic guitar, the string will be held in by a peg on the bridge of the guitar. Remove this peg (you will need pliers). When replacing the string, start by inserting the circular stopper into the hole, and then push in the peg (hard!) on top of it.

2 Winding the string

From now on, all instructions are the same for both electric and steel string guitars.

a Twist the peg of the string you are changing so that the hole on the machine head faces down the neck of the guitar. Insert the new string in the hole, so that is taught, and the pull the string back, towards you, to create roughly 7cm of 'slack'. Add a little more slack for the thinner strings.

b With your right hand, push down slightly on the string. This will create a little bit of tension in the string so that it stays in place. Now, as you are looking at the peg, turn it anti-clockwise.

c The string will start to wrap around the machine head as you turn the peg. For the first rotation, the 'excess' on the end should go under the rest of the string. For each subsequent turn, this excess should go above the remainder of the string. This will help to lock the string in place. Try not to let the string overlap itself, as this may make it easier to break. You may now want to use a string winder to finish off the job.

3 Tune up

It goes without saying, but you will need to tune the string up to the correct pitch. Be aware that the string will slip in pitch, possibly for the first 10 minutes or so, before settling on a steadier pitch. Once you are content that the string is secure and relatively in tune, cut off the excess with pliers or wire cutters **d**.

In conclusion

Congratulations on completing this guitar method – hopefully your playing has really improved as a result, and you feel much more confident with your instrument.

These are the techniques we've looked at in this book – keep practising them and they will serve you well in the future!

The basics
- Tuning the guitar
- Sitting and standing with the guitar
- Connecting an electric guitar
- to an amplifier
- How to use a capo

Scales
- C major scale
- G major scale
- Minor Pentatonic scale
- Blues scale

Lead playing
- Playing runs
- Creating your own runs
- Soloing with the blues scale
- Slides
- Hammer-ons

Chords
- Major chords
- Minor chords
- 7 chords
- Power chords

Rhythm guitar
- Strumming Patterns, using eighth-notes and sixteenth notes
- Arpeggio-style playing
- Creating your own arpeggio patterns

You should be at the stage now where you can start learning some simple TAB transcriptions, and building up a repertoire of songs.

You will find a selection of useful songbooks, TAB books and further guitar methods listed on the next page.

You will also find extra resources available on **musicroom.com.**

1 2 3 4 5 6 7 8 9

HOW TO DOWNLOAD YOUR MUSIC TRACKS

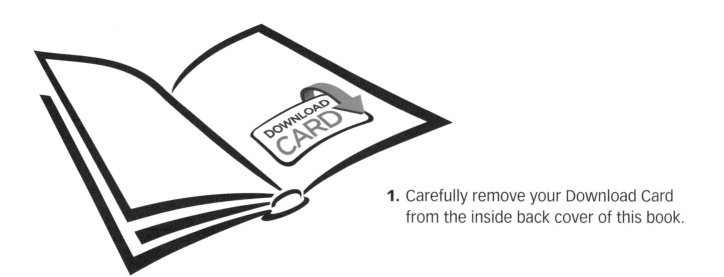

1. Carefully remove your Download Card from the inside back cover of this book.

2. On the back of the card is your unique access code. Enter this at www.musicsalesdownloads.com

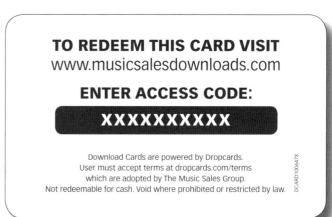

TO REDEEM THIS CARD VISIT
www.musicsalesdownloads.com

ENTER ACCESS CODE:

XXXXXXXXX

Download Cards are powered by Dropcards.
User must accept terms at dropcards.com/terms
which are adopted by The Music Sales Group.
Not redeemable for cash. Void where prohibited or restricted by law.

DCARD1006478

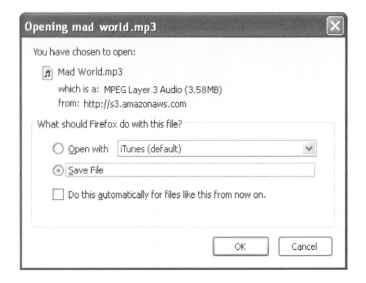

3. Follow the instructions to save your files to your computer*. That's it!

*Appearance of download manager will vary depending upon operating system and web browser.
In case of difficulty when downloading files, please contact dropcards.com/help
Card missing? Please contact music@musicsales.co.uk